TRAVEL WITH THE GREAT EXPLORERS

Explore with

Leif Eriksson

Natalie Hyde

Crabtree Publishing Company
www.crabtreebooks.com

Crabtree Publishing Company
www.crabtreebooks.com

Author: Natalie Hyde
**Publishing plan research
   and development:** Reagan Miller
Editors: Shannon Welbourn
Proofreader: Wendy Scavuzzo
Managing Editor: Tim Cooke
Designer: Lynne Lennon
Picture Manager: Sophie Mortimer
Design Manager: Keith Davis
Editorial Director: Lindsey Lowe
Children's Publisher: Anne O'Daly
**Production coordinator
   and prepress technician:** Tammy McGarr
Print coordinator: Katherine Berti

Produced by Brown Bear Books for
Crabtree Publishing Company

Photographs
Front Cover: Bridgeman Art Library: Look and Learn main;
Superstock: cr; Shutterstock: br; Thinkstock: istockphoto tr.

Interior: Alamy: All Canada Photos 17b, 28-29t, Ivy Close Images
26-27, Danita Delimont 21b, Tor Eigeland 29b, North Wind
Picture Archives, 27t, The Print Collector 10-11; Dreamstime: 20;
istockphoto: 13b; Mary Evans Picture Library: 25r; Public Domain:
19t, 22, Algkalv 6-7, Crow in a Cage 15b, Einar Jonsson, Smallbones
11r, National Museum of Art, Architecture and Design, Oslo 5b;
Craig A. Rodway: 17cr; Shutterstock: 5t, 13t, 15t, 20t, 21t, 23tl,
Steve Allen 18, City Escapes 7b, John A Davis 14br, Andrrzej
Gibasiewicz 18-19, Joe Gough 7t, Imfoto 14bl, Sergey Krasnoshchoko
23b, Sundraw Photography 25cl, TT Studio 4, Zimowa 28:
Thinkstock: istockphoto 10, 24, 27b.

All other artwork and maps © **Brown Bear Books Ltd.**

Brown Bear Books has made every attempt to contact the
copyright holder. If you have any information please contact
licensing@brownbearbooks.co.uk

Library and Archives Canada Cataloguing in Publication

Hyde, Natalie, 1963-, author
      Explore with Leif Eriksson / Natalie Hyde.

(Travel with the great explorers)
Includes index.
Issued in print and electronic formats.
ISBN 978-0-7787-1427-9 (bound).--ISBN 978-0-7787-1433-0 (pbk.).--
ISBN 978-1-4271-7584-7 (pdf).--ISBN 978-1-4271-7578-6 (html)

      1. Leiv Eiriksson, -approximately 1020--Juvenile literature.
2. Explorers--Scandinavia--Biography--Juvenile literature.
3. Explorers--North America--Biography--Juvenile literature.
4. Vikings--Juvenile literature. 5. North America--Discovery and
exploration--Norse--Juvenile literature. I. Title.

E105.L47H93 2014   j970.01'3092   C2014-903660-4
                                                C2014-903661-2

Library of Congress Cataloging-in-Publication Data

Hyde, Natalie, 1963-
 Explore with Leif Eriksson / Natalie.
      pages cm. -- (Travel with the great explorers)
 Includes index.
 ISBN 978-0-7787-1427-9 (reinforced library binding) --
 ISBN 978-0-7787-1433-0 (pbk.) --
 ISBN 978-1-4271-7584-7 (electronic pdf) --
 ISBN 978-1-4271-7578-6 (electronic html)
 1. Leiv Eiriksson, -approximately 1020--Juvenile literature. 2.
America--Discovery and exploration--Norse--Juvenile literature. 3.
Explorers--America--Biography--Juvenile literature. 4. Explorers--
Scandanavia--Biography--Juvenile literature. 5. Vikings--Juvenile
literature. I. Title.
 E105.L47H94 2015
 970.01'3092--dc23
                                                2014020430

Crabtree Publishing Company

www.crabtreebooks.com   1-800-387-7650

Printed in Hong Kong/082014/BK20140613

**Published in Canada
Crabtree Publishing**
616 Welland Ave.
St. Catharines, ON
L2M 5V6

**Published in the United States
Crabtree Publishing**
PMB 59051
350 Fifth Avenue, 59th Floor
New York, New York 10118

**Published in the United Kingdom
Crabtree Publishing**
Maritime House
Basin Road North, Hove
BN41 1WR

**Published in Australia
Crabtree Publishing**
3 Charles Street
Coburg North
VIC, 3058

CONTENTS

Meet the Boss

Vikings spent their summers going 'a-Viking', meaning on expeditions. So Leif Eriksson was following in the footsteps of his ancestors as he explored new lands.

LAND OF FIRE AND ICE

- ☛ Volcanic Country
- ☛ Viking Home Away from Home

Leif was born in Iceland around 970. His family had moved there from Norway. Iceland is called the land of fire and ice, because it has many volcanoes and **glaciers**. The conditions are tough, but so were the Vikings. Most Viking settlers were farmers from Norway. They raised animals and traded with mainland Europe.

FATHER FIGURE

- \+ Explorer Follows in Father's Footsteps
- \+ Outlaw Flees the Law

Leif's father was an explorer himself. He was named Erik the Red, probably because of the color of his hair. He had been **exiled** from Norway to Iceland. When Erik the Red was exiled from Iceland as well, he sailed to Greenland and founded the first Viking settlement.

TRAVEL UPDATE

All Aboard with Lucky Leif

★ All sailors like a lucky captain—and Leif Eriksson was one of the luckiest. While on a voyage, Leif observed a ship get wrecked on an island, so he saved the crew. In return, he was given the **cargo** and he got the nickname, "Leif the Lucky."

Did you know?

The Vikings came from what are now the European countries of Denmark, Sweden, and Norway. They later headed west and settled in Iceland and Greenland.

IMPRESSING THE ELDERS

★ **Young man makes an impression**

When he was a teenager out sailing, Leif saw a polar bear cub on an **ice floe**. Leif sailed "upstream" from the ice floe, then let the strong current carry his boat back so he could capture the cub. Then he used the current to carry him back to shore. It was clear to everyone that he already had great sailing skills.

LET'S GO SAILING

+ **Young Vikings Learn Sea Skills**

Vikings lived, worked, and traveled on the sea. Leif and the other boys hung out at the docks when they were done with their studies and listened to sailors' stories. All boys were taught sailing and ship-building skills. Leif also gained his knowledge by helping his father and brothers.

Where Are We Heading?

Leif Eriksson was already an experienced navigator by the time he sailed to North America. He had visited many of the islands where the Vikings had settled and where they traded.

HOME SWEET HOME
★ You're My Best Friend!

As a young boy in Iceland, Leif followed the Viking custom of living for a few years with another family. Tykir, who has been called Leif's "foster father," taught the boy reading and how to use weapons. At the age of eight, Leif moved to Greenland.

IT DOESN'T LOOK VERY GREEN TO ME!
☛ Travelers head into wilderness

When Leif was about 12 years old, his father founded a settlement in Greenland. The ocean crossing was dangerous and many boats sank. This may be where Leif learned how to sail at sea. While in Greenland, he heard stories of a sailor named Bjarni Herjolfsson, who claimed to have found a new land to the west.

THE LOVE BOAT

★ **Explorer loses his way— and loses his heart**

In 999, Leif sailed to Norway to visit King Olaf I. On the way, he was blown off course. Stranded for nearly a month on the Hebrides Islands off what is now Scotland, he met and fell in love with Thorgunna. She was a noblewoman and daughter of the island's chief. Thorgunna later gave birth to their son after Leif had already sailed for Norway. She named him Thorgils.

MAN ON A MISSION

+ Leif Turns to God

Around 1000, Leif visited with King Olaf I in Norway. Unlike most Viking people who worshiped many different gods, the king had become **Christian**, and urged Leif to become a Christian as well. When Leif left, the king asked him to spread **Christianity** in Greenland.

> And I am confident that fortune will smile on you."
> *King Olaf I to Leif Eriksson.*

WHAT SORT OF NAME IS THAT?

☛ **Explorer Reaches "Helluland"**

Leif wanted to find the land Bjarni had described. He may even have used Bjarni's boat. Leif sailed west until he saw a place covered in rocks. He named it Helluland. Then he sailed south to a shore covered in forests that he called Markland. Finally he landed in a place of grape vines he called Vinland.

Viking Voyages to North America

Viking sailors had already crossed the North Atlantic as far as Greenland before Leif Eriksson sailed to North America. Other adventurers followed his route to explore the new territory of Vinland.

Markland

Markland meant "Forest Land" in the Old Norse language the Vikings spoke. Leif named it because it had many woods beyond its white beaches. His men cut down trees there to take to Greenland.

L'Anse aux Meadows

In 1960, archaeologists found the remains of a Viking village at the northern tip of the island of Newfoundland. It was probably established as a base for exploration by Leif Eriksson or one of the other Viking explorers.

Baffin Island

Hudson Bay

NORTH AMERICA

Labrador

Vinland

Archaeologists think that Leif gave the name Vinland, or "Vine Land," to the island of Newfoundland. His men found grapes growing wild there; the Viking **sagas** said that the grapes made good wine.

Helluland

The first part of North America Leif reached was full of flat stones. He named it Helluland, or "Land of Flat Stones." It was probably part of Baffin Island.

Greenland

Leif's father, Erik the Red, was one of the first Vikings to settle on Greenland. He also gave its name to encourage settlers to move there. In reality, the soil was poor and farming was difficult.

Eastern Settlement

The Vikings lived in two areas of Greenland. The larger one was near its southern tip. It was called the Eastern Settlement.

Iceland

The Vikings began to settle in Iceland at the end of the 10th century. Leif Eriksson was born there, but moved to Greenland when his father was sent into exile for killing a man.

Greenland

Iceland

Newfoundland

England

EUROPE

N

NW

NE

W

E

SW

SE

S

Locator map

Key

········► Erik the Red, 985

———► Bjarni Herjolfsson, 985-986

– – –► Leif Eriksson, 1000

– – –► Thorfinn Karlsefni, 1005

Meet the Crew

Leif grew up listening to the stories of Viking ancestors who had discovered new lands in the past. In turn, he inspired others to follow in his footsteps and set out on voyages of discovery.

 Weather Forecast

NEW LAND FOUND!

As a result of being blown off course, Bjarni Herjolfsson said he saw new land west of Greenland. He was anxious to get home to visit his parents in Greenland, so he did not go ashore to take a closer look. Bjarni's stories, however, inspired Leif to explore the new area.

ALL THAT WAY... TO GET KILLED

☞ **Explorer's brother never comes home**

Thorvald Eriksson was Leif's brother. Thorvald wanted to repeat Leif's voyage to Vinland, even though Leif refused to join him. Thorvald took a crew of 30 men and spent the winter of 1004 at Leif's camp. But the Vikings clashed with the native people, whom they called Skraelings. Thorvald was killed in a **skirmish**. He was the first European to die in North America.

Did you know?

The Vikings loved stories. They wrote down the adventures of Leif Eriksson and the tales of other heroes in long stories known as sagas.

THREE IN A ROW

★ Another Eriksson goes abroad

Thorstein Eriksson was the youngest son of Erik the Red. After hearing what had happened to Thorvald in Vinland, he set out to bring his brother's body home. Thorstein and most of his crew fell ill. They became disoriented in the dangerous open seas, never making it to Vinland. Thorstein died of an illness shortly after he returned to Greenland.

> "People will call us fools for starting off on this voyage, we who have never been in the Greenland seas!"
> *Bjarni Herjolfsson, The Greenland Saga.*

My Explorer Journal

★ Leif Eriksson refused to join his brother Thorvald to make a second voyage to Vinland. Imagine you are Leif and write a letter to Thorvald explaining why you have had enough of overseas exploration.

VIKINGS ON THE MOVE

☞ First settler is another Eriksson... nearly!

After Thorstein Eriksson's death, Thorfinn Karlsefni married Thorstein's widow, Gudrid. They led a large group of people to make a permanent settlement at Leif's camp in L'Anse aux Meadows, in what is now Newfoundland. Gudrid had a son there, named Snorri. After only a few years, however, native attacks forced the group to abandon the settlement and return to Greenland.

Check Out the Ride

The Vikings were master shipbuilders and sailors. Their strong and fast ships helped the Vikings cross the open seas to reach distant lands.

LOOK OUT FOR THE LONGSHIPS

☛ Lean, mean, fighting machines

Did you know?

Sailors on Viking ships kept their personal items in wooden chests. They used these as seats when they were rowing.

Viking longships—*langskip*—were made for warfare. They were long and narrow to sail quickly through the water. The **hull** was shallow, so they could even sail up shallow rivers. This allowed them to get close to villages for raiding, then make a quick escape. Along each side were holes to put oars through for rowing.

SLOW BOATS FOR CARGO

+ Explorers' ships lack luxuries

Traders and explorers often used a ship called a *knarr*. It was powered by oars and a square sail. Part of the deck was covered to protect cargo. This made it more comfortable for explorers, who could take shelter from bad weather on long trips.

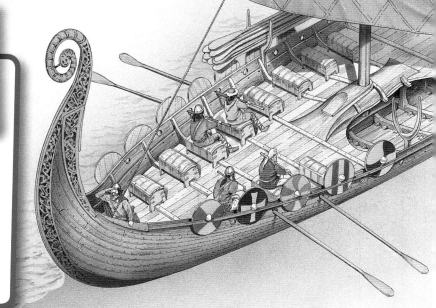

TRAVEL UPDATE

Life onboard

★ Life was hard on Viking ships. The crew slept on the deck using blankets or sleeping bags to cover themselves for warmth. They kept everything in wooden chests. The Vikings were experts at preserving food, and ate dried or salted meat.

Two Ends

A longship had two identical ends. That meant it could be sailed in either direction without having to be turned around. That was useful in narrow rivers.

My Explorer Journal

★ The journey from Greenland to Newfoundland in a knarr would take about two months. Describe some of the animals, landforms, and weather you might see on your journey.

DRAGON'S HEAD

★ We're not scary

★ Dragon gives wrong impression

Drekars were longships with carvings on the **prow** of dangerous animals such as dragons or snakes. People used to think these **figureheads** were meant to scare the Vikings' enemies. In fact, they were probably meant to protect the ship and its crew from harm—and from the monsters the Vikings believed lived in the sea.

Solve It with Science

Follow Me

The Vikings were the best sailors in Europe. They sailed all the way to northern France, the Mediterranean Sea, and even the Black Sea near Turkey.

The advanced sailing knowledge and technology of the Vikings allowed explorers like Leif Eriksson to navigate long distances and survive harsh conditions.

HAS ANYONE SEEN THE SUN?

☛ **Amazing stone finds the way**

☛ **Makes it easy to find the sun**

Vikings used a number of tools to navigate. The *pelorus* was a bit like a **compass**. A bearing dial was a tool that traced shadows to figure out how high the sun was. This kept them in the right position north and south. Vikings also used something called a sunstone. It was made of Icelandic spar. This mineral changed color in the light and helped sailors to find where the sun was in the sky if it was cloudy or foggy.

TWINKLE, TWINKLE...

+ Star helps sailors at night

At night, Viking sailors navigated by using the North Star, also called Polaris. They measured how high above the horizon the North Star was. By comparing that to the same measurements taken at home, they could figure out their **latitude**, or how far they were north or south of the equator.

THICK AS A PLANK

★ **Shipbuilders make stronger hulls**

★ **Ridges add stability**

The Vikings built their boats using *lapstrake*, or clinker-building. In this technique, the planks in the hull overlapped each other. That made the hull strong, and the ridges created by the planks also made boats more stable. Animal hair or yarn dipped in tar filled in the gaps between planks to make the ship watertight.

FORGING NOT A CRIME

☛ **Heavy metal masters**

The Vikings were masters of metal **forging**. Their swords, knives, and axes were made of good quality steel, so they were strong and flexible. These tools were essential for Leif and other explorers to find food, build shelters and protect themselves on expeditions.

TRAVEL UPDATE

Finding the way

★ While sailing close to land, you could watch for landmarks on the coast. Studying birds could tell you if you were close to shore. Some sailors kept a crow in a cage onboard in case they got lost. They let the crow go and followed it: it would fly toward the closest land.

Hanging at Home

Vikings were famous for their brutal raids and violent behavior. But the truth was that most Vikings were peaceful farmers and lived a simple life on the land with their families.

Homestead

Viking homes were often isolated farms. They had a longhouse to live in and many outbuildings, such as barns, workshops, and even bathhouses.

THE MIDDLE OF NOWHERE

+ Living on the edge of the world

Leif's family and the other settlers had a harsh life in Greenland. Trees for building were scarce, and livestock ate all the plants, so the soil **eroded**. Over the years, the temperatures got colder and it became harder and harder to farm. Sea ice closed trade routes and the Greenland Vikings felt very isolated.

ALL TOGETHER

★ **Families share one room**

★ **Who's going to mow the roof?**

Viking houses were usually one large room shared by a family. The roofs were covered in chunks of sod to keep the houses warm. Benches along the walls were used for sleeping, eating, and sitting. In the center was a fire used for heat, light, and cooking.

HOME AWAY FROM HOME

- Viking outpost
- First longhouse in America

The remains of a temporary Viking settlement were found near L'Anse aux Meadows in Newfoundland. According to the Viking sagas, this is *Leifsbudir*, or "Leif's Camp." Leif and later Viking visitors built everything they needed to live comfortably. The camp had several houses, a few workshops, and even a smithy for making metal tools.

IT'S NOT ALL WAR

★ Viking fun and games

★ Great game, crazy name

Although the Vikings worked hard, they also made time for fun. They held feasts to celebrate trading, raids, or weddings. Musicians played flutes and panpipes. During the long winters between explorations, many Vikings played a board game called *Hnefatafl*. It was quite similar to playing chess.

Did you know?

The Vikings used skis to get around and for hunting. They even worshiped the god and goddess of skiing, Ullr and Skadi.

The First Explorers

Exploration came naturally to the Vikings. Leif Eriksson was not the first explorer to head west. Each sailor who went before him added a step toward the final voyage to North America.

 Weather Forecast

STORMY WEATHER

Often new land was found when sailors lost their way. Gunnbjörn Ulfsson was blown off course in the early to mid-10th century on the way to Iceland. He saw a group of small islands and a much bigger landmass we now know as Greenland.

Did you know?

Settlers in Greenland relied on the sea for their food. They caught fish, but they also trapped animals such as seals and seabirds.

GO WEST YOUNG MAN

☞ Exile leads the way to a new island

☞ New capital founded

Ingolf Arnarson left Norway in 874 and moved to a new island everyone was talking about: Iceland. He threw household goods overboard to see where they washed ashore. He found them and settled at what is now the capital, Reykjavik.

ERIK GOES INTO EXILE (AGAIN)

+ Convinces settlers to move to Greenland

When Leif's father Erik was sent into exile from Iceland, he headed for the land Gunnbjörn Ulfsson had seen. After spending three years of exile in Greenland, Erik sailed back to Iceland. He convinced about 500 men and women in 25 ships to set sail with their livestock and families and settle with him along Greenland's deep *fjords* and green valleys.

My Explorer Journal

★ Erik the Red gave Greenland its name to make it more attractive to settlers. Look up pictures of Greenland online, then try to write an advertisement for Greenland that makes it seem as attractive as possible to settlers.

Dead End

Viking settlement in Greenland lasted until 1500. The weather grew colder and the winters were harder. The people eventually moved away.

ERIK'S ISLAND

★ Settlers head east and west

★ Neighbors split up

In Greenland, Erik the Red's settlers split into two groups. Erik became a chieftain in southern Greenland near what is now Qassiarsuk. The rest sailed on to a fjord in the northwest near the modern capital, Nuuk. The two areas were known as the East and West settlements.

Meeting and Greeting

The Vikings did not have a high opinion of native peoples. They called them Skraelings, which meant "weaklings" or "savages." Relations with the Skraelings soon turned bad.

LET'S SWAP

☛ **Trading with the Skraelings**

☛ **Native peoples lack weapons**

At first, the Skraelings in Vinland seemed eager to trade with the Viking settlers. They traded badger furs in return for red cloth and for milk from the settlers' cattle. The natives also wanted the settlers' steel weapons. They only had **flint** spears and catapults.

UNDER ATTACK

+ **Native warriors attack Vikings**

+ **Explorer's brother killed!**

When Leif's brother Thorvald was living in Vinland, his group was attacked by Skraelings paddling canoes made from animal skins. In the fight, Thorvald was so badly wounded he knew he would die. He asked to be buried with a cross at his head and one at his feet. The site has never been identified. The survivors left for Greenland after the burial.

IT'S A RAID!

★ **Bellowing bull saves settlers**

★ **Will the raiders be back?**

Things turned violent when the Skraelings tried to steal the settlers' weapons. They were scared off by the sound of the Vikings' bull bellowing, but the Vikings knew they would be back. The next attacks left two Vikings and four Skraelings dead. Even though the fighting continued, the settlers stayed at Leifsbudir for two more years.

Did you know?

Newfoundland is a large island off the coast of Canada. When the Vikings arrived, people had been living there for at least 3,000 years.

My Explorer Journal

★ **The Vikings thought the Skraelings were very aggressive. Imagine you are a Skraeling. How do you think you would have reacted to the newcomers?**

MYSTERY PEOPLE

☛ **Who were the Skraelings?**

The Skraelings were described in the sagas as small, with coarse hair, large eyes, and broad cheekbones. Archaeologists are not certain who they were. They may have been Thule or Dorset Inuit. They may have also been the Beothuk, a native population who lived in Newfoundland until 1829.

I Love Nature

The Vikings were the first Europeans to set foot on North America. They found plants and animals that no Europeans had ever seen before—and some that were already familiar.

Rich Land

Newfoundland was rich in sources of food. There were plenty of fish and birds to catch, caribou and other mammals to hunt, and berries to eat.

WHAT'S THAT WHEAT?

☛ Rye grows wild

The Vikings were surprised to find "wild wheat" growing in Vinland. Experts think this might have been wild rye. It often grows in woodlands where grapes and butternuts also grow.

THAT SOUNDS NUTS!

+ Butternut clue to explorers' movements

Butternuts are a type of walnut tree. They did not grow in Newfoundland. They needed warmer temperatures from farther south. Three butternuts and butternut wood have been found at L'Anse aux Meadows in Newfoundland. Butternuts do not float, so they could not have floated there by sea. It is believed that settlers brought them north on one of their trips.

EXPLORER FINDS VINES

★ Grapes give name to land

The Greenland Saga explains that when Leif was at his camp in Vinland, his foster-father Tykir came back one day with wild grapes. Tykir explained that this new place was full of them. Leif and his men filled their boat with the grapes and the vines to take back to Greenland with them.

WILDLIFE CORNER

+ **Rivers thick with salmon**

+ **Headlands full of caribou**

The sagas tell of Vinland being rich in salmon in the rivers, flat fish in the oceans, and "dyr" thick on the headlands. Historians think the "dyr" were caribou. The Vikings in North America depended on finding enough food to eat. They also needed to stock up on food before the long voyage home. Lots of meat and fish were extremely important for survival.

> "There was no lack of salmon either in the river or in the lake, and it was bigger salmon than they had ever seen."
>
> *The Greenland Saga*

Fortune Hunting

The Vikings were daring explorers. They were always looking for new places where they could settle or seize goods. They sailed deep into Russia and even to the Mediterranean Sea.

TALL TREES ARE TIP-TOP

- Where would we be without wood?
- Timber used for everything

Timber was an important material for the Vikings. Many of the cold climate areas where Vikings settled did not have a lot of trees. The few that did grow in Iceland or Greenland were quickly used up. House walls, benches, and roof beams were all made of wood. Even more vital was the need for wood for shipbuilding. Expeditions were looking for new and better sources of timber.

ROOM TO LIVE

★ Land-hungry Vikings raid Europe

★ Desperate measures taken

The Vikings were always looking for new territory. Most of the land in northern areas had poor soil and a short growing season. It could not provide enough food to support a lot of people. As the population grew, new farmland was needed.

JEWEL BOX

- Tree resin makes glowing stone
- Amber used for jewelry

One of the most important trade goods for the Vikings was amber. This was a hard, clear material formed by resin from trees millions of years ago. It came in different shades of orange and gold. The Vikings used it to make jewelry. It was popular everywhere, so the Vikings traded it for other goods.

MAKE A NAME FOR YOURSELF

★ Explorers love fame and honor
★ Sagas tell of great feats

For the Vikings, fortune was not only about making money. They also wanted to earn fame. Men went on adventures and expeditions so that the stories of their deeds would be remembered in the sagas. *The Greenland Saga* and *The Saga of Erik the Red* tell the stories of Leif Eriksson and his family.

Did you know?

Vikings believed three Women of Destiny chose a person's time of death at their birth. Because nothing could change this, Vikings were not afraid to live dangerously.

SELL, SELL, SELL, BUY, BUY, BUY

+ Vikings are Europe's top traders

The Vikings had a vast trade network. They traded all over Europe. The timber, furs, grapes, and vines that Leif collected in Vinland could be sold back in Greenland, Iceland or even farther away. The Viking network reached as far east as Russia, where their ships sailed far inland up the mighty rivers.

This Isn't What It Said in the Brochure

Leif Eriksson and the other Vikings who traveled to North America were used to hardship. But even they found settling in the new world they found too much of a challenge.

A BAD OMEN?

- Superstitious seafarer stays home
- Erik gives up on voyage

Vikings were very superstitious. Leif tried to get his father, Erik the Red, to sail west with him. But on the way to the ship, Erik was thrown from his horse and injured. He believed it was a bad **omen** and refused to go on the journey.

 Weather Forecast

SEA GOD CAUSES STORMS

Aegir was the god of the sea in Viking legends. They worshiped and feared him. They believed he came to the surface of the oceans to take ships and men back down to his hall at the bottom of the sea. If a storm blew up, sailors threw valued possessions into the sea as offerings, so that Aegir would be pleased and the storm would end.

My Explorer Journal

★ When sailors were caught in a storm, they often made sacrifices by throwing possessions into the sea for Aegir, the sea god. If you were caught in a storm, what would you throw into the sea?

UNFRIENDLY WELCOME

★ **Natives drive settlers away**

★ **Skraelings too fierce to subdue**

When the Vikings settled in Iceland and Greenland, they either drove away anyone living there or took them as slaves. The Skraelings in Vinland were not so easily dealt with. They attacked the settlers constantly to make them move back to Greenland.

Exposed

In the northern seas where Vikings sailed, storms and sudden rain squalls were common. The open deck of a longship was a miserable place to be.

TRAVEL UPDATE

A Long Cold Journey

★ Viking ships were not made for comfort. Travelers and crew did not even have a sheltered spot to sleep. The open deck meant they got wet and cold when the weather turned stormy. There was also no place to cook and no fires were allowed. Food was eaten cold.

End of the Road

After finding Vinland, Leif was done with exploring but his stories inspired others to try to find the fabled land. In the end, however, the Vikings gave up on North America.

ONCE IS ENOUGH

- Leif stays at home
- Spreads his faith in Greenland

After Leif's voyage to Vinland, he decided not to return. He stayed in Greenland and taught Christianity. Leif was last mentioned in the sagas as being alive around 1019. By 1025, his son Thorkell had replaced him as local chief, so Leif had probably died.

THE LAST VOYAGER

★ Bishop sails into the sunset

In 1121, almost 100 years after Leif Eriksson, the Bishop of Greenland, Erik Gnupsson, sailed for Vinland. He wanted to convert the Skraelings to Christianity. But he was never seen again.

THERE'S NOTHING HERE

- ☛ Vikings give up on Vinland
- ☛ No future for North America

Thorfinn Karlsefni and the other settlers only stayed in Vinland for a few years. They sailed home in 1003 or 1004. That was the last Viking attempt to settle in North America. Thorfinn first returned to Greenland, but later settled in Iceland.

Did you know?

After the Vikings left Vinland, no more Europeans arrived in North America until the Spanish explorer Christopher Columbus reached the Caribbean—about 500 years later!

LET'S TRY AGAIN

+ 20th-century rerun

Some people did not believe that the Vikings could have sailed from Greenland to Newfoundland using only their small ships. In 1998, a group built an exact **replica** of a Viking *knarr*. They named it *Snorri* for the first European child born in North America. Using only the sun and stars for navigation, one sail, and oars, they made the trip in just two months, proving it was easily possible for Leif and his successors to have reached North America.

GLOSSARY

cargo The goods that are carried on a ship

Christian Describing a person who believes in Jesus Christ

Christianity A religion based on belief in Jesus Christ and his teachings

compass A device used for navigation; it has a needle that always points to the north

eroded Wore away by the wind or rain

exiled When a person is thrown out of his or her own country, usually as a punishment

figureheads Designs carved at the prow of a ship, often featuring the head of a person or a creature

fjords Long, narrow, and deep inlets of the sea between high cliffs

flint A type of stone that was chipped into flakes to make points for weapons

forging Making a metal object by heating metal in a fire and hammering it into shape

glaciers Large, thick sheets of ice that move very slowly over land

hull The bottom part of a boat or ship that sits in the water

ice floe A flat piece of ice floating in the ocean, often together with many other ice floes

omen A sign that predicts good luck or bad luck

prow The pointed front part of a ship above water; a longship has two prows because the ship is designed symmetrically to sail either way

replica An exact copy of something

sagas Long stories that are often accounts of historical events; the Vikings told sagas long before they wrote them down

skirmish A small fight between small groups of warriors

Leif Eriksson is born in Iceland around 970 C.E. His father is the explorer Erik the Red.

Leif sets sail for Norway but is blown off course and lands in the Hebrides Islands.

Leif returns to Greenland to spread the message of Christianity.

Leif discovers Helluland, Markland, and Vinland.

970 All dates are approximate

982

999

1000

1003

Leif and his family move to Greenland when Erik the Red is exiled from Iceland. Erik later sets up a settlement there.

Leif sails on to Norway and stays with King Olaf I.

Leif leads an expedition to find the lands described by Bjarni Herjolfsson.

ON THE WEB

www.bbc.co.uk/schools/ primaryhistory/vikings/
The BBC's guide to the Vikings for kids, with games, videos, and fun facts.

www.easyscienceforkids. com/?s=leif+eriksson&submit. x=0&submit.y=0
Facts and quizzes about Leif Eriksson, including a video from the History Channel.

www.ducksters.com/history/middle_ ages_vikings.php
Information on the Vikings including a map and a quiz.

www.pbs.org/wgbh/nova/vikings/
PBS site on the Vikings with links to videos, maps, and other resources.

BOOKS

Bankston, John. *Leif Erickson* (Junior Biography from Ancient Civilizations). Mitchell Lane Publishers Inc., 2013.

Berger, Gilda. *The Real Vikings: Craftsmen, Traders, and Fearsome Raiders*. National Geographic Children's Books, 2003.

Guillain, Charlotte. *Vikings* (Fierce Fighters). Raintree, 2011.

Margeson, Susan. *Viking*. DK Eyewitness Books, 2009.

Richardson, Hazel. *Life of the Ancient Vikings* (Peoples of the Ancient World). Crabtree Publishing, 2004.

Shuter, Jane. *The Vikings*. Heinemann, 2010.

Leif returns to Greenland. He rescues a crew that has been shipwrecked and gets the nickname "Leif the Lucky."

Thorvald Eriksson is killed in a skirmish with native peoples. The survivors return to Greenland.

Constant attacks by Skraelings force the last Vikings to leave North America.

1004 **1005** **1007** **1010** **1017** **1019**

Leif's brother Thorvald sets out to find Vinland.

Thorfinn Karlsefni, his wife, and many others attempt to settle Vinland.

Leif is mentioned as being alive for the last time in the sagas; he probably dies around this time.

INDEX